# Staring at the Wall for Hours

*The Torn Heart of a Pastor's Wife*

L. Cassie Keys

ISBN 979-8-89243-909-1 (paperback)
ISBN 979-8-89526-958-9 (hardcover)
ISBN 979-8-89243-910-7 (digital)

Copyright © 2024 by L. Cassie Keys

All rights reserved. No part of this publication may be reproduced, distributed, or transmitted in any form or by any means, including photocopying, recording, or other electronic or mechanical methods without the prior written permission of the publisher. For permission requests, solicit the publisher via the address below.

Christian Faith Publishing
832 Park Avenue
Meadville, PA 16335
www.christianfaithpublishing.com

Printed in the United States of America

I dedicate this book to my dad and mom, Johnnie and Mattie, my dear sisters, Linda and Vanessa, my children, Jon and Malika, my grandchildren, Jace, Anissa, Zeena and Jaleel and a special dedication to my Aunt Christine.

Thank you to every pastor, ministry and counselor that helped me walk through the coldness of the emotional trauma I experienced that birthed this book. I am unable to name you all. Pastor & Mrs. Tommy Marshall your counsel was life-sustaining and the root that spouted the start of my deliverance and survival in a newfound life- thank you. Pastor Lovy Elias your teachings, prayers and labor in the Word of God caught me at the end of this journey and gave me answers to the hard questions that plagued my soul- thank you (God will give me nations, Taleo). Foremost, with all praises and glory, thank you, my matchless God and King, from whom all blessings flow- if I had 10,000 tongues, I could never praise you enough. I never would have made it without you.

# The Final Day

It was a warm spring day. I was at home when the deceiver came in and then went back out. He was on the phone with a friend from his home state of Texas. I overheard him telling his friend the same lies he had been telling everyone else.

I walked outside and confronted him, asking, "Why are you telling people things about me that are not true?"

He replied, "I told you if you did not stop playing for that community choir, I would do this." (I later discovered he was telling people that I was a musician at a gay club, which was also a lie).

I stormed into the house. When he came in, I confronted him again. The confrontation became heated, and before I knew it, I threw the ironing board, which was sitting open between us, clear across the living room and against the fireplace. As the ironing board hit the wall, I was in his face with the intention of hurting him. I caught myself and just stood there, looking at him with hot, fiery, angry eyes.

I looked him straight in the eyes and said, "You know what? I do not need to be here." It was at that point I finally ended sixteen years of pure hell. As it ended in my mind, he instantly became detached from my heart and life forever. In a flash, I was free from loving him unconditionally. It was time to get out of this misery of a tainted hoax of a marriage. It was time to walk out.

It was the final day in this mess of a life with this sorry excuse of a man. It was the final day in this wicked portrayal of a relationship. It was the final day of sixteen years in a facade of a marriage. When a man is not honest, not truthful, and not in love with you for real, his true colors eventually come shining through, and they did like the sun. It was not clear at first, but soon in the marriage, things started to be noticed. However, I ignored the signs; or maybe I was just naive, trying to do the right thing—stay. Maybe I was just plain stupid. God gives warnings sometimes in dreams. He gave me a warning. I was not in the frame of mind to catch what God was showing me in this dream:

I was in this beautiful house. It was huge, festive, and lit up with wonderful, bright lights. There was a party with all my family and friends. There was music, laughter, wonderful hors d'oeuvres, and lots of fellowship and stories being told. There were so many people. I was surrounded by wealth, happiness, and love. I went out onto the balcony. It was a beautiful large balcony. I was talking with a man who reminded me of John P. Kee (or maybe it was John P. Kee), and he pulled out a ring and asked me to marry him. I became excited and, in my naive innocence, told him, "Yes!" The next scene was the warning in the dream. He took me off the balcony and down the cliff behind my house. Down and down we went. I looked up toward my house and saw it only get smaller as we went further away. We went so far that the music dimmed, and so did the lights. We went so far until we entered the dark, cold, gray muck and mire. We spiraled down so low until a pit engulfed us.

Oh my God! Why did I not notice this warning? I say that because of this! I went to my hometown to let my family meet the guy who asked me to marry him. This was after the dream. When my sister, Cynda, met him at her house, one of the first things she said was "He reminds me of John P. Kee." This was warning number two. Now, mind you, the real, original John P. Kee, the gospel singer legend, is one of the nicest, most generous people you would want to meet. I think the only reason the persona of him appeared in my dream is because of the love and respect there is for him. Satan knows I am a church musician, a Hammond organist, so he used a gospel-singer persona to get my attention. You know, like a wolf in sheep's clothing. Satan will disguise himself as an angel of light, even in a dream. I now look back and see the total picture. Yet then, I just had to get out.

I started to pray. I told God how I needed to find a place to live that day! I explained how much I could afford. You see, I was working but broke from money being stolen by this idiotic, so-called husband. I was also the one who paid the bulk of the household bills. I was the one who took care of my son, my only child. So I needed something cheap. I left the house in search of this cheap place that I needed so desperately to find that day. I drove around town, looking as my heart started breaking into pieces. Even with the pain of everything crashing around me and upon me, I had this determination to find a place that day.

I left the house in search of a place to live. It had to be one I could afford. I gave myself a three-hundred-dollar budget for a new place. I rode blindly through town, but it was as though I knew where I was going. I went to the east side of town and down this short street I had driven on several times. I saw these ladies putting up a For Rent sign on a duplex apartment. I backed up and parked in front of the duplex.

I greeted the ladies and asked, "How much is the rent for this duplex apartment?"

The elderly lady said, "Three hundred dollars."

I was in awe, for this was the amount I had told God. The elderly lady's name was Mrs. Bassier. Her husband had owned several properties around town that he rented. He had since died, and now she and her children had taken over the rental properties.

I explained to her that I was ending an unhealthy relationship and needed somewhere affordable to live.

Mrs. Bassier looked at me and said, "Well, you have found a place."

I wanted to cry as she gave me the lease to complete. Then I remembered I was still on lease with the rental house I was living in. I had to do something to get out of the present rental house I was in with the deceiver. I took the lease for my new place back to my present place where I was living at that time. Then I prayed, "God, help me. You gave me a new place to live. Now give me favor with this present landlord."

My present landlord was a small-framed Hispanic lady from South America. She did not speak English all that well but well enough to understand most of what was being said to her. She once asked me to help her with learning English so she could become a citizen of this country. I did as time would allow me to. She was genuinely nice, and we became friends of a sort. I did not know how she would respond to my abrupt move, especially since I was late on my rent.

I called her and tearfully explained that I was getting out of this abusive marriage. I told her I had to get a cheaper place to live and would move out by the end of the month. It was spring, the month of May 2011. I apologized to her and almost begged for her mercy because I had to leave so suddenly and unexpectedly. To my utter surprise, she understood and told me to take as much time as I needed. She also agreed to the date I gave her to pay the rent. This gave me a sigh of relief. I now had to begin the grueling task of moving. This was not just a physical move. This move would be a very painful, emotional move that would end life as I knew it. But it had to be done.

I had only a few days to move. It took me days. I went to work all day and moved all night, and I mean all night. It was one, two, three o'clock in the morning, going from one house to the other. It was just me and my little dog, Diamond. I was extremely exhausted. My coworkers saw how tired and depressed I was becoming. They did not know what I was going through. I never told them. I just had to push myself. I had to be out of the old house by a certain date. This was hard, so hard. And the deceiver had the audacity to leave all his things in the house as though he expected me to move his things as well. I moved them, all right. I put televisions, nice coats and clothes, shoes, and all his things—guess where? On the street! Somebody got some nice stuff. At that point, I did not care at all. I just had to get out. I had to get out of that house and away from this joke of a spouse.

In a few days, after moving until the early morning hours and going to work totally exhausted and out of strength, I accepted the help of strangers. These two strangers were my new neighbors. My son was a tremendous help in moving the large appliances. If it had not been for my son and my new neighbors, I would not have made it.

Finally, everything was out, and the previous place I called home was empty and swept completely clean. It was finally done. The move into a new place was finally a reality. Praise God! But where did all the furniture go? I looked around, and all I had was the dinette set and a love seat. That was all I wanted out of the other house. I did not want anything that would remind me of the other house, not even the bed I slept on.

So I slept on the love seat. That is where my little Diamond and I slept. Yes, it was a little too short for my long legs, but I made it work. I just propped my ankles and feet on the armrest and covered myself with a blanket. Little Diamond would sleep next to me or as close to my feet as she could get. I got used to it. After a while, my back would hurt some from being unable to stretch out like I wanted to. My son saw how I was sleeping and gave me an air mattress. It was big and roomy. Once I made it up with sheets and blankets, it looked just like a bed. It gave me room to stretch out and sleep better, with little Diamond sleeping at my feet. This was my bed for some time. I could not afford a bedroom set at the time. Yet I was content for now.

I had my own place. I had my own space. I had peace and quiet. No more putting up with friends that were not my friends. His friends ate my food, used my utilities, disturbed my living space, destroyed my peace, and refused to show respect. They did not contribute in any way. It was me taking care of the household expenses with minimal effort from the other. No more putting up with not being able to keep a clean house. I would often think of getting an additional apartment to have a nice, clean place for me in case I wanted to invite over my friends. Living with a lazy, uncaring slob became embarrassing.

I remember going on a women's retreat in Houston, Texas, with ladies from the church. It was a wonderful retreat, but when I returned, I got a horrible surprise and embarrassment. We made it to my house, where a couple of ladies parked their car. They needed to go to the bathroom and asked if they could use mine. Of course,

I said yes. I cleaned the house well before I left and expected it to still be clean. I went to the door, talking with the ladies, grinning and smiling as we talked about our wonderful trip. All of that ended once I unlocked the door and went in. You could tell he had not been there for days. He left a dog he had gotten from somewhere in the house alone. He did not leave the dog in the backyard or put it up on the back porch or in the washroom. He left the dog to roam the whole house, and that he did. There was urine and feces all over the house—on the rugs, the hardwood floors, and the marble floors in the kitchen. I was speechless. I was horrified. My friends had to carefully step over the dog urine and feces to get to my bathroom. My heart sank in my chest. I had never been so embarrassed. After they left, I cleaned and disinfected the floors all over the house and put the dog out in the backyard.

Somebody said I should have left the mess for him to clean and taken the dog off to some back street and left it there. I currently do not remember why I did not. It was my nature to try to do the right thing, even to my hurt. When I was a young girl, my mother told me I was too nice. I did not understand it then, but now I understand it well. Even to my detriment. As I look back, I can say I am also so trusting, so loving, and so wanting to do the right thing that I often overlook the fact that people are not always trustworthy. That people will intentionally do things and say things to harm you or even destroy you. Why has this been so hard for me to grasp and understand? Maybe because in my childlike mind, everybody should be loving, caring, and tenderhearted toward their neighbor. Is not that how Jesus wants us to be? Or do I live in a fantasy world? The answer could be a little of both, huh?

Yes, it was the final day—the day I woke up and clearly saw that I was in a rotting relationship I was doomed to die in. Finally, the light bulb came on. God spoke to me and through me the day I stated, "I do not need to be here." At that point, God gave me the courage to not just walk out but also run for my very life!

# The Shotgun Duplex Apartment

Let me invite you to my new place, which I lovingly called my shack. I called it that because, from the outside, it did look like a shack. It seriously needed a paint job. The paint on the wood on the outside was peeling and flaking. There were spiderwebs in every corner. It needed new trim around the windows. It looked like a poor person's shack on the outside. Well, I was poor, and it was my shack. But once you passed through the wooden screen door and entered the apartment, you saw the vast opposite. This was what the old people call a shotgun house (well, in my case, a shotgun apartment). When you walked through the front door, you found the living room. It had nice hardwood flooring, nicely painted walls, and, to my surprise, a beautiful fireplace and mantel. The fireplace was closed but still beautiful. Walking straight, you walked into a bedroom. The bedroom also had nice wood flooring and painted walls. There was also a closet for my clothes. As you continued straight to a short, narrow hallway, there was the bathroom to the left. It was small but nice with a tub, a shower, a toilet, and a sink with a medicine cabinet above and a cabinet below. There was also an area for towels. It was small but cute and had enough room for me.

Take one or one and a half steps out of the bathroom, turn left, and take one more step, then you were in another room. It was very roomy and had a closet. This was a second bedroom, but it would be my dining room. I was able to keep my dinette set. It was a genuinely nice set with a glass tabletop and a big wooden base made in the design of a modern sculpture. The chairs were high-back chairs with woven wicker-like designs and a soft, upholstered seat beige in color. The dinette set also came with a curio for the dishes, napkins, silverware, or anything else it could hold. It was the nicest room in the apartment. It was the only one with furniture.

Next, we walk into the kitchen. It was a large kitchen with lots of room and cabinets for me. I did have dishes, cookware, utensils, and silverware. I had my own refrigerator, but the kitchen was equipped with a refrigerator and a stove. I brought along my microwave and other kitchen gadgets. So my kitchen was full of all the necessities. Outside of the kitchen was the washroom, stocked with my washer, dryer, and small deep freezer. I also used this last room for storage. Then, lastly, the back door. So from the front door, if you walked straight, you went right through the house and straight to the back door, like right through the barrel of a shotgun. Still, it was now my new home.

As happy as I was to get moved and settled in my new apartment, even with just the essentials I owned, it proved to be a time of thoughts, tiredness, and tears. It would be a time of loneliness, lack, and lethargy. I went through the deepest agony ever in my life. I did not understand how trying to do the right things could throw me into a pit of hell. I could not fathom in my mind why people hated me. Why did they turn their backs on me? Why did they kick me to the curb like a dead animal run over by several cars on a busy street? All I did was show love and compassion. All I did was try to show love to my fellow neighbor. All I did was pray for those who spitefully used me.

Oh my god. My world was spinning out of control! I had been beaten up by the life that was supposed to be a good one. I was the first lady. I was the pastor's wife. I was the one who labored in prayer for my church family. I was the one who tried to hold everything together, including the church. I was even the one who labored in prayer for the pastor, for the one who was not what people thought he was. Do I dare say he was altogether totally different in private? There were things done in private that, even today, I did not personally see but spiritually discerned. Did any of it matter? Was my labor in vain? I was now hanging on for dear life on this cold, chilling death ride. God, please save me.

# The First Dream

As I was going through this ordeal, I suffered a lot of trauma but had no outlet in a person or physical thing. Some would turn to alcohol, cigarettes, drugs, or even an affair. I turned within myself. It was an unconscious inlet, not an outlet. It was like I carried the burdens like a pregnancy for a time, only it was not a baby or child that would be born, or was it? Maybe it was a way for me to go deep inside myself, my inner thoughts, my heart of hearts. It was my hideaway. It was my secret cave. It was my straitjacket in the insane asylum of my soul. Unknowingly, what I was feeling and carrying deep in my psyche was buried so far in me that it could only be shared in some silent way. The shame, the fear of people, and the need to protect myself took over and pushed me further and further inside the secret cave I had decided to hide in, my safe place. It was only in my dreams that I saw what was happening on the inside. It was only in my dreams I could see what happened on the outside. It was my dreams that led me and showed me where I was emotionally. The dreams I am telling you are real. I was moved to journal them, and I did. I started a dream journal.

In my dream journal, the date of this entry is Monday, April 18, 2011, the first day of Passover. It is the first dream. I remember it like it was yesterday. Last night, I dreamed I was on a beach. It was not very bright. It was gray and dark. I went down to the water for someone to take my picture with the ocean behind me. I went down to where the ocean washed up on the beach. The camera would not work. I went to the person who had the camera to see why it would not work. A few seconds after I left the spot where I was standing, I looked around and saw the place where I was standing sink! Then the ocean water rushed into the sunken area with great force. As I watched, I thought, *If I had stood there just a few seconds longer, I would have died.* My heart was filled with fear and concern. I told the people with me to be careful to watch where they put their feet.

Then the dream changed, and I was at a small shop near the beach. As I went in (there were people with me), I saw a room filled with grand pianos! I was like a kid in a candy store. The pianos were black and varied in sizes and length, and some looked like antiques. As I walked and enjoyed seeing so many grand pianos, I noticed one white grand piano. I stood there amazed at its beauty. I tried to take a picture, but the camera would not work. Then the dream changed again.

I was with my sister, Cynda, in my hometown; but it was at Highland Village Apartments, where she lived many years ago. It was as if I went there to stay with her for a while. She was orienting me to her apartment. I sat in the car, then walked up the steps to her apartment. Then the dream went back to the shop with the pianos. My friend Cassandra was playing, and a gospel choir was singing. I tried to take a picture of her, but the camera would not work. The dream then changed again, and a young girl ran to me and said she needed me to come back to the shop. She wanted me to play the piano. I told her I would. Again the dream changed, and I was on my porch at the old house, the house of the last confrontation, mentioned earlier, the house I left in the spring of 2011. I got ready to go back to the shop with the young girl and play the grand piano. As I looked toward the sky, a storm was building. It was getting very dark and windy. I grabbed my umbrella and prepared to leave for the shop. I felt no fear. I just prepared myself to leave in the storm. But, as I remember, it seemed the umbrella I had would not be enough protection for the storm I saw coming, a storm nothing nor anyone could have prepared me for.

# Depression Sets In

I was in the bedroom of my small duplex. There was nothing in the room but boxes, a closet, and the air mattress on which I was sitting. Yes, I was just sitting quietly, not speaking. There was no one to speak with, only my small dog, Diamond. But right then, I could not even speak to her. What did I feel? Nothing. I was just numb, not even feeling the pain that had led me here. I did not feel the crushing or the shame right then. I did not feel the pressure I felt earlier that day at work nor the heat as I drove home from work, the heat of the sun blazing through the windows of my vehicle. I felt nothing—on purpose.

Sadness took place. This sadness was strange. This sadness went so deep that reality turned black. Depression set in with unbearable heaviness. I asked God, "Is this how You feel when we do not love You?" Then I repented, telling God, "Lord, I am sorry." Then came the tears. I was just sitting and staring. Tears were running in a continuous stream down my face. But I was not crying. Crying would cause me to feel. I did not want to feel. I did not want to cry, but I could not stop the tears from rolling. There were so many that these were the overflow. I could not contain them. I could not stop them from flowing. They leaked uncontrollably even though I refused to cry. If I cried, then I would have to feel, and right then I did not want to feel. So tears were just flowing because of the overflow and because my heart was also bleeding. It is an internal bleed from the crushing, a hemorrhage from the shattering of my heart into so many pieces. I could not comprehend the number of pieces. In my mind, I tried to pick the pieces up. I did, but there were so many. And they were so shattered I could not grasp them all. They kept falling from my hands. Please see that I was trying but could not grasp them all. Agony set in.

I was so numb. I could not feel. I could not feel the arrows in my back. I could not feel the lies that tried to taunt me. Or could I? I could not feel the looks of people who, for some reason, then hated me. Or did I? They looked me up and down like I was a piece of trash or a dead animal on the side of the road. Nasty looks from people I did nothing to. Yes, I'd just sit there, numb. I created an amnesia from the people, the shame, and the pain of it all. It was here on this air mattress, in this empty bedroom, in this little duplex, that I found anesthesia. This is where I shut out. This is where I shut down. No one could get in; but, unfortunately, I could not get out. As I sat, I slipped into a stupor. (God, help me), feeling this voice in my head saying, "Just let go. Just leave reality and all this crushing, numbing agony behind."

Time seemed to just slip away, and so did my mind. It wanted to just slip away—away from shame, hurt, and lies. Could I just let go and lose it all, including my mind? I felt my mind slipping. I heard Satan telling me to let go, and I almost let go. They would have said, "The divorce! She lost her mind over the divorce or over him." But never in a million years! Not over filth like him. To lose my mind, to let go, to die, would be giving in to Satan's temptation to die. That was the plan—to kill me, to destroy my name, to ultimately crush me. Wow. It took all the small faith I had left to just breathe—one breath, two breaths, three breaths—just to live as I sat and stared at the wall for hours. For days and weeks in my bedroom, on the air mattress, after work and after church or going to the store, I just sat on the air mattress, staring at the walls for hours, tears flowing.

Then the recurring night terrors began. A man and woman were stalking my shotgun apartment, passing by with murder in their eyes. Their vehicle reminded me of an old army tank with no top, just a skeleton body, adding more fear to the atmosphere. It was like a type of Chaldean war horse, with fire breathing from the nostrils, continually going up and down my street, passing my place and causing horror. Night after night, this terror interrupted my sleep. That was until this particular night when the terror reached a momentous level. Shots were fired from the Chaldean skeleton with ammunition so extreme and deadly that it created enormous holes in my shotgun shack. The holes were so great they appeared as windows, exposing the insides of my once safe home. The fires from the vehicle's nostrils kept coming, seemingly unstoppable, causing tremendous damage to my home. I picked up my little dog in my arms as the ammunition went straight through, chasing me out of my shotgun apartment. I had to run for my life or die in the vicious attack. As I ran outside through the back door, heading into the backyard, I turned to see if more fiery shots of terror were following me. I only remember turning, shaken with trepidation, and running as far and fast as I could while clutching my little dog in my arms.

My mind twitched, ready to slip, and everything went black. No one would know what happened. They might ponder what happened, and that would be once it was discovered I was alone in an empty duplex, on a single air mattress full of tears and the leakage from a bleeding heart. My heart just wanted to stop beating. My heart wanted to feel nothing. My heart wanted to just cease from existence. In all the tempting from the tempter to die, something deep in the spirit, something out of all the pressure, something quiet and still, broke through with just one word, one powerful word: *live*. At that point, the tears did not stop. The pain did not cease, but a decision was made in my soul to live. Worship music filled the void and ministered to my torn heart and soul. This music filled the room I was sitting in. It kept me from tipping the balance negatively into an internal entrapment of death; it held me like a lifeline thrown at the perfect time. While I almost slipped through the cracks of a mental breakdown, the strength of all strengths saved my failing mind. The strength of God.

# The Question Why?

So why did I almost slip into the empty darkness of a mental breakdown? Let's try to answer that question with some questions. In answering my questions, you can see why. Some of the things I was accused of doing were so far-fetched they were obviously lies. But people will believe a lie more than the truth, and this they did. I was even told that the church people would take the side of the pastor because he was that in all his undercover sins—the pastor. I was just the first lady, the pastor's wife. I was the one thrown under the bus and dragged until I fell apart. Here is the question I want you to ponder and answer for me: Were the things I was being accused of the things the other party was doing? My mother once told me when a person is accusing you of something, they are the ones doing that particular thing. I have heard others say the same. I am guessing you are on pins and needles to know what I was accused of, correct? I dare not say; I plead the Fifth. It is not the truth, and I am not going to rehash that demon of a lie. I killed it. Have you ever heard the theme song from the *007* movie, "Live and Let Die"? I will never resurrect it.

I would not speak negatively about him, the other party, although I could have, in truth. Yet he, and the church members that believed his lies, continued to sling me under the bus. Let me ask you this, and again, it is not my intention to attack the character of a person. I am honestly seeking to understand and to be understood. May I ask, especially the men, if your wife is in the bedroom, waiting for you, naked, would you be found in the bedroom across the hall, behind closed doors with the same kind, for hours? This question is for everyone: if you were a pastor of a church, any church, would you spend time together in the housing projects with your alcoholic friend until 2:00 a.m., 3:00 a.m., or 4:00 a.m. while your wife is home alone? First, why are you there all night, Pastor, when nothing but other alcoholics, drug addicts, and prostitutes are always known to run through there? Why are you not home with your family? Or studying the Word of God in preparation to feed your flock? Is it because you were also caught up in the drinking, drugs, and prostitutes? This is maybe the reason there were always complaints of headaches that kept the pastor from his responsibilities in the church, like the Easter Sunday that went on without the pastor at the last minute. Was it due to the guilt from the things done the night before, when you stayed out doing your secret stuff in the housing projects? How about the countless Wednesday Bible classes you were too sick to go and teach? Who was the one who did it? The first lady, the pastor's wife.

What about the church members that turned against me, the same ones, like your youth director, whose phone calls you saw on your call ID and simply ignored or gave to me to answer. Even calls from your bishop. I would watch as call after call was ignored and statements like "I do not want to talk with him," or "I do not want to talk with her," were made with a look of disgust. But everyone was fooled. This was a master manipulator and a two-faced liar. I pray repentance has occurred. Perpetrators can only last for a little while before God uncovers everything. I was almost caught up in this thing, this snare, like a bird in a fowler's trap. But God delivered me. Have you ever been in a snare? Have you ever been tricked and captured with seemingly honest intentions that were later found to be evil devices to harm, even destroy, you? I have.

# I Missed It

I had to admit to myself that I missed it. I missed the signs God showed me. I missed the warnings through the dream and other signals. I was naive and not in a place of strategic discernment. I had my head in the clouds and did not see through the cloudiness how God was warning me. This was a hard pill for me to swallow. When I realized my mistake, it hit me like an aluminum bat on the head. I missed it. This led me down a path of seeking to know and clearly see the signs, warnings, and signals God gives us concerning how to move forward with the decisions in our lives. I began to seek God's wisdom.

In the King James Bible, Hebrews 12:1 states, "Wherefore seeing we also are compassed about with so great a cloud of witnesses, let us lay aside every weight, and the sin which doth so easily beset us, and let us run with patience the race that is set before us." This scripture is one of the deciding tools God used to give me comfort and peace in my decision to leave. This is what grasped me. The definition of *besetting sin*, according to the Google Oxford Languages dictionary, is "a sin that a person struggles with the most, and that they find difficult to overcome." Could my sin have been my involvement with the spouse who beset me? The word *beset* is defined in the dictionary as "to attack on all sides, assault, or to harass." This definition spoke volumes. It made all the sense in the world. This gave me peace in my decision to leave simply because I was being attacked on all sides and harassed. The verbal assaults were as damaging as any physical assault could have been. The evil intentions and lies were attacks and assaults of great magnitude. They were an attempt to murder me emotionally and spiritually. The Word of God broke through the cloudiness of my mind and said, "Listen to God. God is saying, 'Lay it aside. It has beset you. Lay it aside!'"

# My Plea to You

I pray you can learn from the mistakes I made. Helping you has helped me. Helping you helped me understand why I stayed when the relationship became toxic. At first, I did not see it as toxic. My heart was so full of God's love; all I wanted to do was be an example of love like God loves me—unconditional love. But His Word, in Matthew 7:6, says, "Give not that which is holy unto the dogs, neither cast ye your pearls before swine, lest they trample them under their feet, and turn again and rend you." In other words, do not waste good things on people who will not appreciate them. They will step all over you like a rug, then turn on you to tear you to pieces. Sometimes innocence and humility must be balanced with wisdom and self-preservation. In other words, do not be a fool. Protect your heart, for out of it flows the issues of life (ref. Proverbs 4:23). Do not let anyone suck you dry. Do not let some unworthy man or woman kill you emotionally, mentally, and spiritually. Any person who is low enough to do that to someone who only shows them love and patience is an extremely dangerous person with no consciousness of God, a wolf in sheep's clothing. Beware, my friend. Be wise as serpents and innocent as doves—with a concentration on the wise aspect. Be like Christ—gentle in spirit yet strong and steadfast in wisdom, discipline, and discernment.

If you are in a place such as I was, please, my sister or my brother, do not die in this situation. Do not lose your self-worth or your self-esteem. Please save yourself! *Please save yourself!* Do not lose your identity in Christ, your self-worth, or your self-esteem. Do not let anyone tear you down. Please know God does not intend for us to be ignorant (unknowing, naive). Open your eyes. See the signs. See

## STARING AT THE WALL FOR HOURS

the way of escape. Please, my sister or my brother, if you find yourself in any type of toxic relational situation, see the signs God is showing you. Don't ignore the signs. When God opens a way of escape or gives you a word of liberation, run for your life!

# Enlightenment

In listening to ministers, counselors, and preachers and in reading several books, trying to figure out if something was wrong with me, one sermon hit home like no other. Now, through the years after the divorce, I was greatly helped, encouraged, and given strength and wisdom for the times of those present days through the ministry of great ministries and books by anointed authors. I was immensely empowered to move forward. Yet there is a word for this present day, only a few days ago, a word that cultivated the heart's soil even greater. It answered an ongoing question that had been plaguing my mind for years: Why do I love people to my destruction, my dissatisfaction, and often to the demise of my character? Even when I disapprove of negative actions toward me, why do I just take it? Do I have a sign on my back stating, "Kick me"? Again, I asked, "What is wrong with me?"

On this particular day in November 2023, I listened to a sermon that answered my questions. It was not that I did not know or had not heard in the past the biblical teaching topic the man of God taught this day. It was like what the Bible states as a word in due season.

> A man hath joy by the answer of his mouth: and
> a word spoken in due season, how good is it!
> (Proverbs 15:23 KJV)

This word was simple. Gold. Yes, gold! In the sermon, the minister taught concerning three elements of the earth: wood, silver, and gold. He described so eloquently the characteristics of each of these elements. He had my total attention. I was like a baby bird being fed a worm by its parents. Then the enlightenment happened. When he described the characteristics of gold, my attention was replaced by awe. I was moved to tears.

This man of God described the characteristics of gold with so much wisdom and knowledge, yet even a child would understand it. My awe, amazement, and to-tears moment happened because as he described the properties and attributes of gold, he was describing… me. He did not mention my name or look at me through the TV and point me out. I was mesmerized as God spoke to me through his sermon. It was life-changing. For he stated these things that stood out the most:

> Gold adds value to anything it is connected to or added to; if you add gold to the elements wood or silver, gold makes the wood and silver more valuable because gold is more valuable than both. Then he stated that even through the value, worth, and weight of gold, it has a flaw. It is soft, leaving it vulnerable. Gold has to be mixed with silver to make it more solid and stronger, even though gold is more valuable than silver.
> (Dr. Lovy Elias, paraphrased)

The word that stands out to me is *value*. The value of gold.

God said to me, "You are valuable. You are not naive or stupid. You are just gold. You add value to the wood and silver of your life. Those people, situations, and questions, even in your own mind, that made you feel small were just wood and silver that tried to demean you, but it was you who added value to those people, places, and positions. It was your value that changed the atmosphere in so many rooms. It was your value that covered the church during your numerous Friday nights locked up in the church in prayer. It was your value that held the marriage together as long as it lasted. It was your value that showed unconditional love even when you were hated for no reason. It was your value that protected you from the deceitful lies that were told about you, even the ones you do not even know about." God told me that day how valuable I was.

I needed to be strengthened. I needed to mix with the silver experiences in my life to establish myself. I needed to even be connected and combined with the wood of my life to give it value. It was never about me. It was about my godly assignment: to love God and people. Jesus had this same assignment, and he did it unto the shame of the cross. So this shame, hurt, and buffeting I went through is not even comparable to what my Savior endured.

I am okay now. I understand now. My head is no longer in the clouds. I have wisdom now. I have the strength to move forward. Thank God for this man of God who had an assignment to teach that word on that day that I watched. God is utterly amazing, and just one word from the throne of God is all we need for a life-changing experience.

You, my brother and my sister, are valuable. You are gold. You add value to every place you go, to everyone you meet, and to every situation. You are stronger than you realize, even when connected to or covering the wood and silver of your life. Walk in the Word of God. Speak the Word over your life and over those connected to you. Know how valuable you are. Believe me, you are valuable. Your big heart does not make you dumb, stupid, crazy, or any of the ugly, negative names a person may try to tag on you. I only hope you can see, as I saw, that you are valuable. I cannot say it enough. This is what has encouraged me just in the last few weeks. I smile now from the inside out. Oh, how I want this for you.

I am not staring at the wall for hours anymore. I am praising God with every ounce of being I have, and I am doing so for the rest of my life. No more darkness. No more tears of pain, agony, and defeat. Now my tears are for the joy of the one word that broke through my spirit way back on that air mattress. That word kept me from slipping quietly away as I sat there with a bleeding heart and a tear-saturated soul, staring at the wall for hours. That word was *live*. I speak life to you. I say to you, "Live."

# About the Author

L. Cassie Keys, was born and raised in Montgomery, Alabama. She has also lived in Georgia (Atlanta, Carrollton) and Texas (Beaumont). She has traveled throughout the United States and abroad to countries such as Japan, Africa, and the Bahamas as an accomplished Hammond organist, pianist, and songwriter. As an author, her greatest desire and mission are to ameliorate and encourage as many people as possible.

Printed in the USA
CPSIA information can be obtained
at www.ICGtesting.com
LVHW040159031124
795419LV00001B/176